A STEP-BY-STEP BOOK ABOUT
GERBILS

PATRICK BRADLEY
HEATHER PENCE

Photography: Michael Gilroy, Ray Hanson, D. G. Robinson Jr., Glen S. Axelrod.
Humorous drawings by Andrew Prendimano.

Distributed in the UNITED STATES by T.F.H. Publications, Inc., One T.F.H. Plaza, Neptune City, NJ 07753; in CANADA to the Pet Trade by H & L Pet Supplies Inc., 27 Kingston Crescent, Kitchener, Ontario N2B 2T6; Rolf C. Hagen Ltd., 3225 Sartelon Street, Montreal 382 Quebec; in CANADA to the Book Trade by Macmillan of Canada (A Division of Canada Publishing Corporation), 164 Commander Boulevard, Agincourt, Ontario M1S 3C7; in ENGLAND by T.F.H. Publications Limited, Cliveden House/Priors Way/Bray, Maidenhead, Berkshire SL6 2HP, England; in AUSTRALIA AND THE SOUTH PACIFIC by T.F.H. (Australia) Pty. Ltd., Box 149, Brookvale 2100 N.S.W., Australia; in NEW ZEALAND by Ross Haines & Son, Ltd., 18 Monmouth Street, Grey Lynn, Auckland 2, New Zealand; in SINGAPORE AND MALAYSIA by MPH Distributors (S) Pte., Ltd., 601 Sims Drive, #03/07/21, Singapore 1438; in the PHILIPPINES by Bio-Research, 5 Lippay Street, San Lorenzo Village, Makati Rizal; in SOUTH AFRICA by Multipet Pty. Ltd., 30 Turners Avenue, Durban 4001. Published by T.F.H. Publications, Inc. Manufactured in the United States of America by T.F.H. Publications, Inc.

CONTENTS

INTRODUCTION

There are many very common animals in pet stores and zoos about which little is known. One reason for this may be that even though these animals are common they have not been studied extensively. Such an example is the gerbil. Gerbils are a very attractive, popular pet with large dark eyes and a furry tail, but they have only recently been studied in any detail. In fact, their systematics was worked out during this century. They were first discovered in China and later introduced to the United States by Dr. Victor Schwentker for use in scientific experiments in 1954. Gerbils are still being used extensively in scientific research and a fair amount of information concerning rodent-carried diseases has been accumulated which is very beneficial to humans. Gerbils are one group of rodents which in nature do not generally carry diseases that are detrimental to humans. Other more basic research has also been done concerning their behavior and taxonomy. Gerbils have many interesting behaviors, which is one of the many reasons they are so popular as pets. They are also interesting from a taxonomic (systematic) point of view. They have a fairly definite range of habitat and demonstrate many interesting adaptations to the areas in which they live. For this reason many scientists who study the relationships that similar species possess have devoted a considerable amount of time to the study of gerbil systematics.

Systematics

The gerbil is a member of the kingdom Animalia, phylum Chordata, subphylum Vertebrata, class Mammalia, order Rodentia, suborder Myomorpha, family Muridae (or Cricetidae),

FACING PAGE:
Stocking stuffer? Gerbils make wonderful pets, but always plan carefully for the acquisition of any animal.

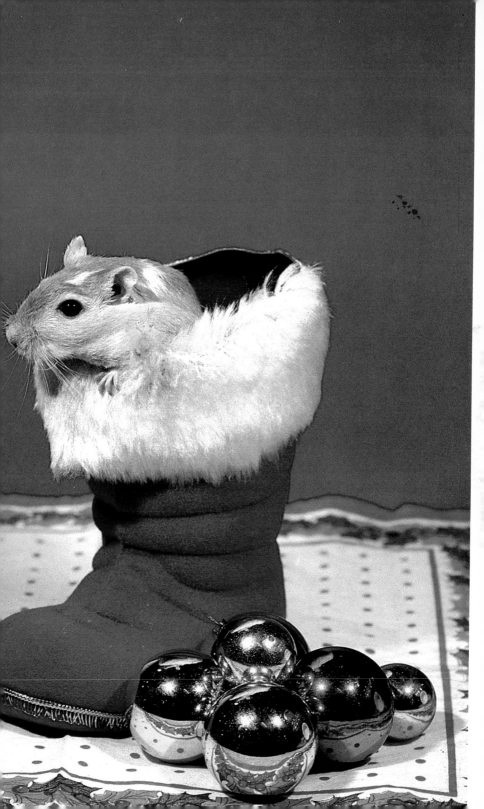

and subfamily Gerbillinae. In the subfamily Gerbillinae there are 15 different genera and 81 species. Many characteristics of gerbils are the same characters that distinguish rodents from other mammals. The word rodent comes from the Latin, *rodere*, to gnaw. Rodents are distinguished by the arrangement of teeth that allow them to gnaw. There is a pair of front teeth in the upper jaw and a corresponding pair in the lower jaw. These teeth grow continuously throughout the life of the gerbil. The teeth maintain a uniform length by wearing off at the tips during daily use. Since these teeth work against each other, if one is dislodged or lost, the other will grow unchecked and cause serious damage to the individual. Closer examination of the mouths of rodents in general shows that most mouse-like rodents have the continuously growing incisors and chewing molars. Between these teeth there are no other teeth, and the space is referred to as the diastema. Normally in this space the canines and premolars are found. The squirrel- and cavy-like ro-

Gerbils forage for food at night and sleep during the day in the wild.

Gerbils need to use their teeth regularly in order to avoid overgrowth.

dents possess one or two premolars on each side. Within the placental mammals, the rodents have the greatest diversity of morphologies, number of species, and modes of life.

Habitat

Rodents are found throughout the world; however, gerbils are known only from specific areas. All reports confirm they are found in North Africa across the Middle East and into China. One source reports gerbils from the pampas of South America. The South American variety may represent rodents being introduced centuries ago by ships sailing between Africa and South America, or they may date back to the separation of the continents.

One consistent feature of the gerbil's range is the climate. Gerbils dwell in hot, arid, almost desertlike areas. These areas are characterized by very hot, dry days, and often cold nights. Water and food are very scarce in these areas, and owing to this, gerbils have developed a plethora of adaptations that allow them to deal with these limitations. One physiological adaptation is the development of cells that store water. The colon is also very efficient at reabsorbing water; for this reason the feces of gerbils are very dry.

Behaviorally, gerbils have also developed adaptations to deal with their harsh environment. Two such behaviors are tunneling and becoming somewhat nocturnal. Gerbils hunt and move around at night and retreat below the surface into tunnels during the day, where they are shielded from the hot, dry heat. Below the surface it is cooler and more humid, very similar to the phenomenon found in caves. The humidity can be controlled to some extent by the gerbil in this situation. The tunnel has many openings and by closing some of these openings the humidity may be increased. Humidity can be increased further by the gerbil sweating. The humidity has a twofold importance: first, it helps in an area where water is limited and second, increased humidity lowers the temperature.

Another adaptation is the storing of food, a behavior found in many mammals. Gerbils feed primarily on seeds and roots, which provide nutrition and, to a lesser extent, water. The seeds collected at night are permeated with dew, so by bringing them into the humid tunnel, the water held in the seed is improved. Once again, though the water in the roots and seeds is minimal, it is important in an area where water is a limiting factor.

Morphology

In many ways, gerbils resemble field mice and small rats due to their general shape and cryptic coloration. However, they have certain features that make them easily distinguishable from other rodents. Some of these characteristics are a slightly abbreviated snout (unlike most mice and rats which have longer, extended snouts) and tails with hair along the entire length and a tuft on the end. Two of the most distinctive features of gerbils are their back feet and legs. Their back legs are comparatively large and muscular, making their running motion more like hopping than running and reminiscent of a kangaroo.

One other characteristic of gerbils that is not readily noticeable has to do with their ears. The lobe structure is normal, not large and not small, but inside there is a very large

It may be a good idea to keep two or more gerbils, as they are social and communal animals.

tympanic bullae. This large area gives the gerbil remarkable hearing ability. This ability is an important antipredator mechanism for an organism that lives in an open area. Along with their extraordinary hearing ability, gerbils also have very large eyes, an adaptation found in many nocturnal organisms.

Thermoregulation

A way by which many temperate zone animals conserve energy during periods when activity is not possible is by entering some form of hibernation or torpor. This drops the animal's metabolism, thereby conserving energy until activity is possible again. This phenomenon is pretty well documented in rodents in northern climates. A less known activity is estivation. For most purposes this is the opposite of hibernation. In estivation the animal retreats to some type of den when it is hot, and its metabolism slows down. Gerbils exhibit both estivation and torpor, depending on the species and habitat. Gerbils from very hot desert climates estivate on a daily basis, denning up during the day and hunting by night. The energy saved by this type of behavioral and physiological response to the heat can be quite substantial, since it is energetically much more expensive to cool off in very hot weather than it is to warm up in very cold weather. This is similar but opposite to the torpor phenomenon documented by researchers dealing with field mice in the New England area. Gerbils from temperate to colder climates, such as the Mongolian gerbils, may use torpor as a way to conserve energy. These types of phenomenon, torpor and estivation, are what make gerbils so fascinating to research scientists.

These wild Mongolian gerbils will warn each other of approaching danger by drumming their feet on the ground.

Introduction

Gerbils are naturally curious and friendly.

Life History

Gerbils have a life expectancy of usually three years, but some reports discuss gerbils living as long as five years. Females enter estrous every four to ten days. Gestation lasts on the average 25 to 28 days depending on the species of gerbil. Newborn, or pups, are naked and blind at birth and are usually weaned after 21 days. After birth the pups can be left in the same cage with the parents, usually with no problems. Depending on the species and climate, females may give birth to two or three litters a year.

Gerbil Behavior

The popularity of gerbils as pets is probably due to their natural curiosity. In many instances where most other animals might turn and run, gerbils will advance to investigate. This is a very pleasing characteristic in a pet. Gerbils are often found standing on their hind legs with their noses in the air, investigating the surroundings. They also possess some curious forms of communication. Like many rodents, gerbils are often heard making squeaking noises in the presence of other gerbils or when startled. One other behavior that is peculiar to them is thumping. The gerbil will thump its back leg as a form of communication in connection with courtship displays, playing, and as an alarm signal. There are numerous studies currently being conducted in an attempt to understand these behaviors and to better comprehend the way gerbils survive in the wild.

GERBILS AS PETS

If asked, most people would probably consider the gerbil to be an attractive pet rodent. They have large, dark eyes and furry tails. When asked to describe a gerbil, most would describe the Mongolian gerbil (*Meriones unguiculatus*), since it is the most common in pet stores, and for that reason will be the one considered in this book. Males average about four inches in length (nose to base of tail), and weigh about four ounces; females tend to be a little smaller.

The gerbil's size and temperament make it an ideal pet. The Mongolian gerbil, like other gerbils, is very inquisitive and not known for biting without provocation. As long as they do not feel threatened, they will allow you to pick them up or pet them; this process will be described in detail later.

Gerbils love to poke their noses into new things (below). They may even stand on their hind legs to get a better view (facing page).

Another factor that makes gerbils desirable pets is their natural cleanliness which stems from their need to conserve water in the wild. Since they have adapted to an environment where water is limiting, water is removed from their food by the digestive tract very efficiently, so little is lost in feces. The kidneys also retain water, producing only a few drops of concentrated urine. This helps to minimize the amount of cleaning required in maintaining your gerbil's cage. It may be one of the most attractive features of a gerbil as a pet.

If you are considering a gerbil as a pet, there are three basic places you can find them. The first would be out in the wild. This means the more arid areas of Africa and Asia. For

A cinnamon mother keeping an eye on her six-week-old daughter.

Gerbil markings appear at an early age.

this reason, capturing a gerbil in the wild for a pet is probably not a very good idea. The second place is from a breeder. Gerbil breeders are not very easy to find unless you are familiar with the pet breeding industry. The third possibility, and the best way to go about getting a gerbil, is by going to a pet store. Pet stores generally have a wide selection of animals and accessories for your pet. Thus you can purchase a gerbil and all the necessary equipment for maintaining the animal at the same time. The operator of the pet store should be able to offer suggestions about care, feeding, and housing or provide you with another source for this information.

The main reason for acquiring a gerbil as a pet is because you like animals and want to get one you will enjoy. Gerbils have great potential for being a very enjoyable animal. They are pleasant to look at, cute and furry, easy to hold, four inches and four ounces, and have a very even temperament. The last point, about their temperament, is often one of the most important features to many people. The reason is because people buy these animals for children, and an even-tempered animal that is not easily provoked to biting is important if it is meant to come in contact with children.

HANDLING GERBILS

Probably the first thing you are going to want to do is to play with the gerbil after you purchase it. This may not be a very good idea. Gerbils are naturally curious, but during the process of being chosen at the store and taken home, the animal may be slightly traumatized. For this reason there are some precautions that should be taken, starting immediately after purchasing the gerbil. First: If the animal is purchased at the pet store, which is the best place to get one, the pet store salesperson will probably give you a container to transport it home. If you also bought a cage for the gerbil at the store, then it can be transported in that, but be sure to add some shredded paper to cushion the ride. This also will allow the gerbil to set up a temporary nest for the ride home. This is important because the less the gerbil is disturbed the easier it will be to handle it when you get it home.

Second: When the gerbil is home do not try to handle it right away. If the gerbil was brought home in a container it should be relatively easy to introduce the pet into its cage; just try to do it as gently as possible. Information on handling gerbils without touching them will be described shortly. Once the gerbil is in its cage it will be easy to observe that it is naturally curious, and this is a plus because it makes it easier for you and the animal to get acquainted. Give the gerbil a day or so to get acclimated to its new surroundings, then introduce your hand very slowly and steadily into the cage with the gerbil; do not make any sudden motions. The gerbil will come over to investigate the new addition to its territory. Mostly it will just sniff and probably crawl over your hand if possible. It may attempt to gnaw at your hand; do not become alarmed and jerk your

FACING PAGE:
Some people create a natural setting in their gerbil's cage in order to make their pet feel more at home.

hand away because the animal probably will not gnaw hard enough to break the skin. If the gnawing does bother you, just withdraw your hand slowly. By going through this ritual on a regular basis it will make it possible for you to pick up the gerbil without alarming it.

Using food as a way to break the ice is a good idea. Put a small amount of sunflower seeds in the palm of your hand and then rest your hand on the floor of the cage so the gerbil can crawl into it. When the gerbil is comfortable in your palm you should be able to reach in and pet it with your other hand (one finger should be enough). Do not follow this ritual every time because the gerbil will become used to it. This means the

As a rule, commercial gerbil products would be safer for your pet than would this homemade obstacle course. Gerbils, because of their long tails, should *never* be given treading wheels.

Handling Gerbils

Let your gerbil get accustomed to you before handling him.

gerbil will begin to associate your hand with sunflower seeds and may accidentally bite you looking for seeds. A lot of accidents at zoos and pet stores are the result of animals becoming habituated to routines. They begin to associate people and peoples' hands with food and only food, so whenever a hand is introduced into range of the animal's mouth it gets bitten. So try to avoid this type of situation. Eventually your gerbil will get to know you and will allow you to pick him up without an in-

It is a good idea for both children and adults to learn the correct way to hold a gerbil.

centive. However, offering it sunflower seeds from time to time is always a good way to keep the lines of communication open, but sunflower seeds should be given in moderation. Holding your gerbil is fine and is something you should do, but in moderation and with care. The most important thing is to be gentle whenever handling your pet. Remember, this is a small animal, and you can easily hurt it if you squeeze too hard, and this may cause the gerbil to retaliate by biting.

Third: *Never* pick the gerbil up by the tail. Some spe-

Persistence is the better part of valor, as this gerbil finally makes his way up the tunnel.

Handling Gerbils

cies of gerbils have very fragile tails. It is believed this is an anti-predator mechanism. On many gerbils their body fur and the fur on most of the tail is all one color, but the tuft at the end of the tail is another color. Some researchers believe this tuft may act as a lure, causing predators to strike at the tail rather than the body of the gerbil; the tail will then come off. A similar phenomenon is found in some lizards. So if you grab the tail, it may break off. To pick up the gerbil, it is best to let it crawl into your hand; or you can use an empty jar of some kind, but be sure to cover it after the gerbil is inside since they jump rather well. Place the jar on its side in front of the gerbil and allow it to crawl inside, then turn it upright and cover it (make sure air can get inside). You can then carry the gerbil (gently) to wherever you want to release it. All you have to do is repeat the pick-up sequence in reverse. For instance, say you want to clean your gerbil's cage and you do not want to pick the animal up in your hand. Set up a temporary holding tank, taking precaution to make sure it is escape-proof. Then get a glass jar (less chance of jagged edges that could injure the gerbil) and a piece of cardboard or wood to hold over the top once the gerbil is in it. Hold the jar on its side inside the cage housing the gerbil and let the animal crawl inside. Do not chase or harass it into crawling inside the jar; it will eventually crawl inside out of curiousity. Then turn the jar upright, cover it, carry it to the holding cage, and gently tilt it allowing the gerbil to get out.

Fourth: When the gerbil is sleeping, let it sleep. The saying about sleeping dogs is equally appropriate for gerbils: let them lie. Being rudely awakened will just startle the animal and may get you bitten. Remember, the whole idea here is to not traumatize the gerbil, so the best thing to do is just be gentle with it.

As mentioned earlier, the tail (usually the very end) can break off if handled a little too roughly. If this does happen there will be a little blood involved. You may be upset a little, the first time you witness this, but experience has shown that the gerbil will survive. You may want to swab it a little with clear water and you can try bandaging it, but often the gerbil will remove the bandage. The tail may heal with a noticeable scar, but your pet will still live a normal life.

HOUSING

The type of housing you choose for your gerbil really depends a lot on how many animals you have. At first you may have only one, but it is important to realize that the Mongolian gerbil is a communal animal and would probably do best if kept with at least one more. For this reason you may want to get a cage with enough room for at least two gerbils. A cage as large or larger, than a ten- or twenty-gallon aquarium would be best. In fact, aquaria can make good homes for gerbils. There are a number of different holding devices for gerbils available commercially. There are wire, glass, wood, and plastic cages. Whatever type of cage you use, remember that these animals gnaw on practically everything. Many people attempt to build their own enclosures out of wood or plastic; subsequently they find a little hole and no gerbil. Gerbils are well-known for their gnawing ability. So even if you are a very good craftsmen you may want to weigh the pros and cons of building a cage yourself. The best thing to do is look over the selection of cages at the pet store and try one of them.

The different types of gerbil-holding tanks are almost as numerous as the different types of gerbils one can find in nature. They range from simple little plastic boxes with wire lids to large elaborate connected boxes that resemble gerbil apartment complexes. The holding facility you choose will be up to you, but it is always good to have some idea of what is available and what points to consider before making any kind of decision. Gerbils are small animals, but buying the animal, holding tank, and accessories is going to add up to a fair amount of money. For this reason it is good to have an idea of what is involved in housing suggestions for gerbils.

To help, we will attempt to give a quick synopsis of some of the holding tanks you may find in your local pet store. The first holding tank to consider is the simplest. This tank is just a rectangular plastic box (container), somewhat like a shoe box in shape and design but with a wire mesh lid. The lid lifts

Every gerbil cage should contain some toys.

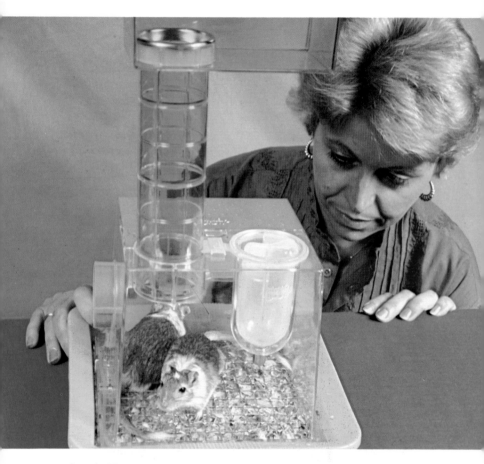

A typical housing set-up for gerbils.

off like that of a shoe box and this is the only way to introduce or retrieve things from the container. The wire lid has two areas in it: one for food and the other for a lick-tube water bottle. As stated this is by far the simplest of holding devices, the most inexpensive, and probably not the one to buy if you intend to keep gerbils in it as pets for any length of time. This set-up is often used in research facilities as temporary holding containers for experimental rodents. They are used in research facilities because they are cost-effective, easy to store when empty or full, and easy to clean. For holding a pet they have certain disadvantages. The first and most obvious problem is that the only way to view the gerbils is through the lid, since most of the containers are opaque. Some come in clear plastic, but are very brittle and fragile. These containers make ideal temporary holding areas for your gerbil when you are cleaning the primary holding facility. They cannot be recommended as a primary

This cage is for exhibition and should not be used as permanent housing.

housing container, but would make very good secondary housing for short periods of time.

The next container is also rather simple in design. It is similar to a holding set-up used by one of the authors of this book while conducting behavioral research on least shrews, *Cryptotis parva*. It has also been described for gerbils, but on a larger scale. What is required is a glass aquarium and dirt. The interesting or attractive feature of this set-up is the way it approximates the natural environment of gerbils, more so than most other settings. When selecting a cage, keep in mind that you will want to give the gerbils an ample substrate to live on. A good substrate is topsoil deep enough for the gerbils to tunnel, which they are innately predisposed to do. Eight inches deep or more of topsoil should be enough for the gerbils to live in. Scattering rocks and sticks on the surface is also a good idea

This is just one style of gerbil cage available; your pet shop probably will have a variety of styles to choose from.

Gerbils will investigate anything in their vicinity.

because the rocks can be set in the soil to help firm up a tunnel and the sticks can be gnawed on to wear down the animals' teeth, which is important. The cage will never truly approximate their wild environment, but any small attempt to do so is encouraged. If the cage is a glass aquarium, the gerbils will probably set their tunnel against the wall which gives you the opportunity to observe them in their tunnel.

Like all other potential set-ups, this one too does have

disadvantages. A few are that it is not easy to handle the gerbils without collapsing their tunnels; if a gerbil dies it is not always obvious, and if there is a breeding pair, pups may get trapped in a collapsed tunnel. This set-up does allow the gerbils the opportunity to tunnel and it does not have to be cleaned often because the urine and feces just get mixed into the soil. A large aquarium also allows the gerbils ample space to move around and get exercise.

Along with the problems of tunnel collapsing possibilities, there are some other not-so-obvious problems. One is concerned with the fact that aquaria are not designed for this purpose. Aquaria are made for fish which live in a three dimensional media more so than gerbils; gerbils are more two dimensional in their orientation. Aquaria are more tall than wide so you lose a lot of space to the unnecessary height. An aquarium that was not quite so high, but a little wider than usual, approximating an equal sided cube would be better and could be made quite esthetically pleasing to the sight. There would still be a ventilation problem since it would be open only

All gerbils love to go in and out of doors. This fellow is waiting for his friend to come out and play.

Gerbils love to climb and explore their surroundings. Be sure to give them some safe, interesting furnishings.

These four are good examples of some color varieties in which gerbils come.

on top. This design has problems, but mostly in regard to the amount of upkeep and initial expenditure of time and money. There will be logistic problems in obtaining the right aquarium, cleaning it and keeping it clean for long periods of time. It will not have to be cleaned very often, but when it does need cleaning, the aquarium and dirt separately are heavy; together they can only be described as cumbersome. Intuitively, this seems to be a great way to go in setting up your gerbils, but it has numerous problems with getting started, maintenance, and it will take up a considerable amount of space.

The next type of gerbil container is one of the most common and popular---a cage with welded wire bars. That is the general description and it has many variations. In general, it is what most people think of when they think of a cage for small animals---little wire bars with a small door. Some of the older models of these are made of all metal with a metal floor that either detaches or slides out for easy cleaning. There is usually a hopper of some kind that is either built to the outside or attaches easily. There is also a place or way to attach a lick-tube water bottle. These come in various sizes and with various attachments or accessories.

Many, instead of being all metal, are a combination of metal and plastic. The bars are metal and sit on top of a plastic rectangular dish or tray. This is a very nice design as far as ease of maintenance is concerned. The cage top attaches to the plastic tray with a series of clamps; when it is time for cleaning, unsnap the clamps, lift off the cage, remove the gerbils, clean the tray, and put the gerbils back. The wire-bar top permits ample ventilation and allows you to watch the gerbils. This may be one of the best designs, and a good cage to seriously consider. The number of variations available with this design are a big plus. There are different sizes, attachment possibilities, tray colors and shapes, and other variables. All in all, a very good

This fellow is marking his territory by rubbing the branch with his scent gland.

The more variety a gerbil is given in his housing, the more fun he will be to watch.

set-up; the only problem is that you do have to be careful to pick a sturdy cage. Make sure all the welds of the welded wire are intact; any small opening and your gerbil will be out. This brings up the space between the bars. Make sure the bars are not spaced too far apart. This is a good point of discussion for you and your pet store owner. Cages designed for larger rodents may have bars that allow too much separation to hold a gerbil. So if you do decide on this design, you need to examine the cages carefully.

One of the last types of housing is an elaborate set of containers connected by tubes. This is a rather unusual set-up because it allows the gerbils a lot of space. This is because it makes use of vertical movement as well as horizontal movement by making tunnels that go up, as well as to the side. So, it is three dimensional rather than being only two dimensional like most animal-holding facilities. This set-up generally is more expensive than most other cages, but since it is composed of many small units it can be bought a little at a time and built up. This is one of the attractive features because buying a little at a time makes the cost seem less. This set-up also provides a lot of variety for your gerbil and you. One of the reasons for having any pet is as a form of companionship and gerbils are no exception, so anything that might enhance this state is a plus, and in some ways the multiple unit housing arrangement for gerbils might do just that. The variety of living areas, or activity areas, allows your gerbils adequate space for moving around and may increase their activity and allow you more opportunity for observing them and their numerous behavior patterns. Like all the other possible housing arrangements this arrangement also has disadvantages. The first has already been touched upon and that is cost---they are not cheap. Second, the ventilation in these containers is not as good as in others. The set-up is made of hard plastic with many holes for air circulation, but it is not nearly as well ventilated as the wire bar cages. Third, they are not hard to clean, but they are not easy. The time spent cleaning depends on the number of units involved; the more units, the more cleaning.

As noted, all the possible types of housing for your gerbils have their pluses and minuses. The decision you make should be an educated one and based on what you are willing to pay and what you are willing to do in the way of maintenance. The best way to do this is to go to a number of different

The tail is one of the gerbil's most distinct features.

pet stores and look around. The list of cages we have just pro-
vided is by no means a comprehensive one. There are a number
of different kinds of cages available at pet stores and it would
not be possible to describe each one here. We hope that we
have given you a general idea of what is available and some
helpful information to keep in mind when looking for a cage.

After you have chosen your cage you will then need to
choose cage accessories. Some of the easiest of choices pertain

to the water and food dispensers. The reason they are easy choices is because there really is not much variety and after you choose a cage, your choice of water bottles and food hoppers is immediately lessened because some cages take only certain hoppers or already have them built in and so on. The same is true in the case of the water bottle.

Another accessory is the bedding for the bottom of the cage. The gerbils will need some kind of substrate to set up their nests. Like cages, there are a number of different types of bedding. We have already discussed soil to some degree in regard to the large aquarium and the potential problems with that. What we did not address was where to get it. One place would be your yard, but then you take the chance of introducing unwanted bugs and other organisms into your home. Sterile topsoil for use in gardens can be purchased at most garden centers and this would be the way to get your soil if you decide to use the soil as bedding. There are numerous other bedding types that are not as time-intensive as soil. Cedar shavings is one type that is very popular. Cedar shavings are used for many rodent pets because the strong natural scent produced by cedar conceals urine and fecal odors which are not a problem with gerbils. Aspen bedding is also very good and has a consistency different from cedar that allows gerbils to burrow to some degree, unlike cedar. There is also pine and dry crushed corn cob. One thing that must be watched with all of these beddings is the amount of dust that can build up. Dust is harmful to all kinds of animals because it can be inhaled and lead to irritation of the lungs and respiratory problems. One way to avoid this is to make sure the bedding is not left in the cage too long; if it is, it will begin to degrade and become powdery. So if you choose to use wood shavings of some description (and this is a good way to go), you may find it necessary to change the bedding every ten days to two weeks. One advantage of using wood shavings is ease of cleaning the cage. You can buy shavings at most pet stores and if you want to buy them in bulk they are usually available at most feed stores.

To help in selecting a cage we have tried to give you a quick synopsis of the possible choices you may find in your local pet store.

NUTRITIONAL NEEDS

Gerbils enjoy sunflower seeds and people love to watch the gerbil manipulate the seed in their front paws and remove the outer shell. Sunflower seeds are a very good source of protein, but they also contain fats and carbohydrates that lead to obesity and an unhealthy gerbil if the fascination of watching the gerbil peel sunflower seeds gets out of hand. Like all other organisms, gerbils have certain nutritional requirements that must be met if the animal is going to lead a healthy life. These nutritional requirements cannot be met by eating one type of food. Sunflower seeds are a good source of protein as mentioned, and should be given to the gerbil in moderation. Just because they have protein does not mean that is the whole story.

The word protein is often bandied around without understanding what it means. A protein is a string of amino acids in a specific order and it is these amino acids that are important. After the protein is broken into its component parts during the digestion process, it is the amino acids that are used by the cells. Plants can produce amino acids from chemicals, but animals must rely on breaking down proteins found in their food. So the fact that sunflower seeds have protein is important, but it is equally important to realize that these proteins do not contain all the necessary amino acids. There are about 22 characterized amino acids at last count and all 22 are not found in every protein.

For the gerbils to be healthy they need a balanced diet just like people. People eat eggs which are a good source of

FACING PAGE:
Gerbils enjoy a balanced diet in the wild; it is therefore important that the owner of a pet gerbil provide a variety of food.

Lettuce, given once in a while, can provide a nice change of pace for your gerbil.

protein containing practically all of the known amino acids, but people cannot live healthy lives on a diet composed entirely of nothing but eggs. The same is true for gerbils; they need a balanced diet composed of a variety of foods. Variety is very important because the exact proportions of amino acids needed is not known, and the way to insure that the gerbil gets the necessary type and quantity of amino acids is to provide it with a variety of amino acids by giving it a number of different foods.

Fats and carbohydrates are also necessary because these provide the energy for breaking down the proteins. Without the fats and carbohydrates, a lot of the proteins taken in would not be broken down and consequently would be wasted. The energy from the fats and carbohydrates is also used to fuel other bodily functions such as the nervous and endocrine systems, and many behaviors necessary to survival could not be

performed. Vitamins and minerals are necessary parts of the diet as well. Without these, many basic cellular functions could not be performed. Calcium is one very obvious need. Bones would become weak without it. Iron is necessary for oxygen transport in the circulatory system. Vitamin deficiencies can lead to numerous diseases (vitamin C scurvy; vitamin D bone diseases; etc.).

The gerbil also needs roughage in its diet or the digestive system will malfunction. Without roughage and fiber, food will not move through the digestive tract properly and the necessary elements cannot be removed from the food.

Given this background information about the nutritional requirements of gerbils, it is time to explain how easy it is to meet these needs. Gerbils have become very popular pets and because of this, prepared food packages are available commercially. They are labeled as gerbil food and the food is almost identical to that of hamster food since their nutritional requirements are very similar. The food is a mixture of grains, nuts, seeds, some egg, and vegetables. These mixtures usually con-

This pair (dove female and agouti Canadian white-spotted male) maintain their beautiful coats and sparkling eyes through eating a balanced diet.

tain all the nutrients gerbils need to remain healthy.

Gerbils can become, for lack of a better word, bored if fed the same mix every day and may stop eating or reduce their eating. Introducing a food they have not had before may solve this problem. Other rodents such as rabbits and rats are fairly popular as pets and there is food made especially for them which can be given to gerbils from time to time. The rat pellets are accepted quite happily by gerbils. Rat pellets are somewhat log-shaped, about an inch long and very hard. These are good for gerbils to gnaw on. Most hard pet foods like dog biscuits are all right for gerbils. As mentioned earlier, it is important to provide gnawing material so the gerbil can wear down and sharpen the front incisor teeth. There is also available commer-

Variety is important in the gerbil diet, but be certain that fruits and vegetables are not given too often.

Nutritional Needs

Sunflower seeds are popular with this ivory female and cinnamon white-spotted male, as they are with almost all gerbils.

cially food known as gerbil treats. These are good for the gerbil, but should be used as treats, not a mainstay of a diet.

Another necessity of the diet is fresh vegetable matter. Any supermarket will carry more than enough variety of these foods. Remember that gerbils in the wild derive a lot of their water from things such as roots. Vegetables also carry many of the necessary minerals and vitamins that are not always found in appropriate quantities in the prepared foods. Broccoli, lettuce, celery, carrots, and other similar foods are good for your gerbil on occasion. Certain garden weeds like dandelions and clover can also be used, but be careful not to use weeds sprayed with insecticide or herbicide. All green foods should be rinsed and fed to the gerbil in limited quantities because too much fresh vegetable matter will make the animal sick.

If you are worried about feeding your gerbil too much vegetable matter, but still want to make sure it is getting enough vitamins then you can add the vitamins to its drinking water. Specially compounded vitamins for this purpose are available at many pet stores.

Keeping the cage clean is very important and the gerbil is not likely to do it. Therefore, it will fall to you to make

This cinnamon gerbil is on his way to dinner. When purchasing a feeding dish, be sure to buy one that is too heavy for the gerbil to tip over.

sure that the cage does not become a breeding place for bacteria that may harm your animal. There are some common sense precautions that will insure that the cage mess does not get out of hand. First concerns the food dish: make it heavy enough so that the gerbils will not turn it over or drag it around. If you buy a cage from the pet store it may come with a built-in hopper so the dish cannot be dragged around. Make water available at all times and use a lick tube water dispenser since these when kept in good condition are the least messy. These come in the form of a bottle that attaches to the side of the cage.

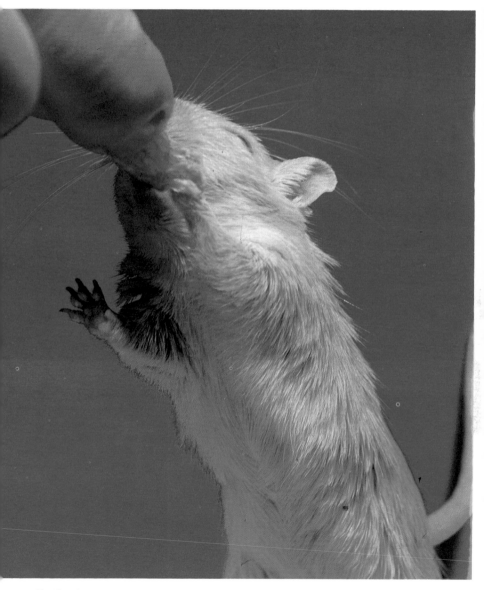

Feeding by hand is a good way to get acquainted with your pet, but be careful not to spoil him.

BREEDING

As mentioned earlier, Mongolian gerbils are communal animals and live in nature in large social groups of one to three adult males, two to seven adult females and several subadults at their maximum. This demonstrates that keeping more than one gerbil is possible, in fact preferable. The gerbils work as a group in their communal living, actually collecting food and storing it for use by the group and defending the territory as a group from other gerbils and strange animals in general.

Inbreeding is a potential problem with communal organisms that can be determined by performing an investigation of the percentage of the group. If the group was perpetuated by breeding within, then inbreeding would definitely cause genetic problems and the group would break down. Studies of gerbils in captivity have worked out the breeding situation in the groups. The social groups remain stable and territorial, so the idea that the breeding takes place by outsiders entering the group is not really viable. When a female enters estrous she leaves her territory to mate and then returns to her own burrow where the offspring are raised under the care of the mother, aunts, and uncles. Some dispersal takes place and new territories are set up, with densities of 20 burrows per acre possible.

This is the case for Mongolian gerbils and not the case for all other species, so it is important to look into what species of gerbil you are buying (Mongolian gerbils are the most common as pets). Other species have different degrees of social liv-

FACING PAGE:
Breeding for color morphs, such as light dove and cinnamon, is becoming more and more prevalent, but more research needs to be done in this field.

A dove and cinnamon pair.

ing. The most desert-oriented species tend to be solitary and the savanna species more communal. This may be a tendency derived from food availability. In the deserts food is more scarce so each gerbil may fend for itself, whereas in savannas food is abundant and collecting as a group is more profitable. Gerbils living in areas with periods of cold weather, such as the Mongolian gerbil, are likely to form complex family social groups. This may be due to the need to huddle together for warmth.

This background information will help in understanding the breeding process. One of the first things to look for, if you plan to breed gerbils, is to find young (two months old) gerbils that are not siblings. If the gerbil is healthy at two months then it should have successfully passed through the stages where any hereditary defects will have surfaced and the most vulnerable time for nonhereditary diseases. At two months the gerbils should be easy to sex, so picking a pair will not be difficult. It may be best to purchase at least two pairs since there is no guarantee that the first pair will be compatible. Gerbils select mates and in the selection process can reject potential mates. It has been found in other rodents that females are capable of detecting inferior mates that may have genetic defects that are not expressed, but which would be expressed in the offspring. Rejection of potential mates for one reason or another is not uncommon. The more pairs that one starts with, the better are the chances of finding two that are compatible, and young gerbils are more adaptable to new situations and will accept the new conditions more easily.

In nature the males are generally larger than females and can be sexed with some confidence by this method, but in

Mating of a dove female and agouti Canadian white-spotted male.

captive-raised gerbils this method is not reliable. Sexing gerbils can be a little tricky because it requires inspecting the genital areas and this is done by turning the gerbil upside down to some degree. To examine the gerbil, the best thing to do is to hold it at the base of the tail and look at the area just before the tail on the underside. The male should have a large nearly hairless patch in this area that is the scrotum, and the female will have no such area. In fact the male will have two areas, one the anal area and the other the scrotal. If time permits, you will notice that both male and female gerbils have two openings. In the female the anus and vagina are fairly close, whereas in the male the scrotum and the anus are further apart. This procedure will need to be carried out quickly because the gerbils will not stay in this position long and will try to thrash free. This can cause serious injury to you and the gerbil. Make sure you hold the very base of the tail; if you hold further down you will damage the tail.

When selecting breeding stock you will want the healthiest possible gerbils. The eyes should be clear, shiny, and black. The fur should be smooth and shiny, without any patchiness, and the tail should be at least three-fourths the length of the body. The tail should be straight, uniformly covered with hair from base to the tuft at the end, and have no kinks. The fur on the body should be uniform all over, dorsal and ventral; there should be no bald or thin patches. If you see a gerbil that has bald patches it is either genetically defective or infected. The legs should have a consistent covering of fur and the nails should be uniform in length and dark in color. Ears should be standing erect and covered on the outside with fur. The body should be inspected for sores; any sores indicate a gerbil that is not healthy due to some disease. Gerbils should be alert due to their inquisitive nature unless they are resting; any gerbil that seems skittish has either been abused or is just not healthy. Make sure you choose a healthy gerbil because any defects may be propagated in the offspring.

Gerbils used to come in only one color, the tannish color (known as agouti) that comes to mind when you think of gerbils. However, since gerbils have become popular pets, other color morphs have been selectively bred. The reason most of

Black female and agouti Canadian white spotted male.

These babies are 24 hours old and white spots are already visible on their heads. Their father is a Canadian white spot.

these other color morphs are not seen in the wild is any deviation from the accepted is usually conspicuous and represents a hazard to the breed. The most obvious example are albinos. Albinos of almost any animal usually are rare because they are easy prey for predators to detect since they contrast so severely with their background. They also suffer from weaknesses in some of their internal organs. Albinos often result from inbreeding practices which are not good procedures to follow if you want to produce healthy strains. Inbreeding tends to increase the chance of expression of deleterious recessive genes. These genes will usually remain unexpressed as long as they are not matched with another recessive; pairing siblings increases the chances of matching recessives.

The genetics of gerbil color morphs is not well studied and colors other than the normal tannish, or agouti, are not common. There are black, but these are rare like albinos, and there are piebald. Piebald can be tan and white piebald or black and white piebald. These are all uncommon when compared to the agouti.

The sexual physiology of gerbils has been well studied and the breeding of gerbils is relatively easy. If they are placed in a cage with ample space and left alone except for feeding and watering, they will breed on their own. If you would like some control over the time of year when they breed, it is good to know that the female gerbil will reach her first estrous at the

A family of albinos. Father is carrying shredded paper to the corner of the cage.

A young breeding pair—black female and agouti Canadian white spot male.

age of 10 to 12 weeks. There is a period of anestrous in which the female will not respond to the sexual advances of the male. As estrous approaches the female experiences an increase in certain hormonal secretions that stimulate the development of the eggs and eventually the release of eggs. The release of the eggs causes other hormones to be secreted that prepare the uterine wall for the implanting of fertilized eggs. Further hormone secretions assist the birthing and nursing process. This is a greatly simplified explanation of the process that the females go through. The process in the males is different owing to an alternate set of hormones and another time schedule for the re-

To sex a gerbil, hold it carefully at the base of the tail.

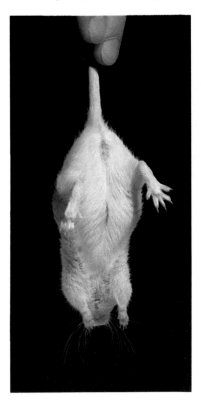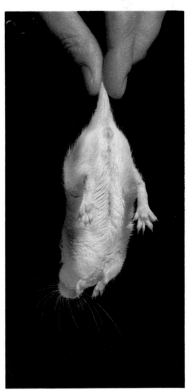

lease of these hormones with the male cycle being a little different. For instance the principle hormone in the female is estrogen, and in the male it is testosterone.

The main breeding period occurs in the midsummer, and midwinter is the time of least activity. This is a generalization since some species have adapted to different environmental pressures. Females are capable of producing more than one litter per year. The reproductive life of a female is about 15 months. A female may enter her next estrous while nursing the current litter. Since the young are weaned in about 21 days and gestation is about 25 to 30 days, this is not a problem. The litters are usually about four to six pups, but litters of eight, and a maximum of up to 12 have been reported. The reproductive peak of a female is reached around one year of age and declines after that. A female older than one year will often produce fewer pups, which are not as healthy. The male's reproductive life is about 20 months with the peak occurring about the same time as the female's.

The act of copulation in gerbils is fairly complex with many components. The female must be in estrous and the male must be at the peak of his sexual cycle. The courtship displays are somewhat intricate with thumping playing a very prominent part. Sniffing of the genitals is important and if the female is receptive she will crouch, exposing her hindquarters, at which time the male will mount her. Ejaculation will not usually take place during the first series of thrusts. The male dismounts, thumps, mounts again thrusting, then repeats this process somewhere around ten times before ejaculation.

After fertilization occurs and the fertilized egg implants in the uterine wall, nest-building activities take place. Pet stores sell materials for gerbils to use in nest-making.

The young are born without fur, poorly developed and with their eyes closed. Nursing starts and this is a good time to change the diet a little to assist the female in nursing. The diet should now consist of a greater proportion of fats, calcium and phosphorous. Sunflowers and fresh vegetables are a good way to do this, but in moderation; only a small increase is necessary. Slowly, but surely, the pups will begin to develop fur and move

These three-week-old babies are already furry and active.

around. By 15 days the eyes are open and the mother will have a hard time keeping the pups in the nest. The male will help to some degree in caring for the nest and pups, but mostly the female assumes the burden.

ILLNESS

Rodents in general are very sturdy animals which accounts for their large numbers worldwide. Gerbils are no exception; they are very hardy and can hold their own in most situations. As mentioned earlier, a well-balanced diet is very important. A diet with a lot of variety that affords the gerbils the opportunity to get the amino acids they need to build proteins is the best way to help them fight off diseases. A healthy gerbil will be much more resistant to illness than one that is malnourished. A clean cage is another way to prevent illness since a clean cage will not be a breeding place for disease-causing bacteria. Gerbils are hardy and are adapted to harsh environments, but do not do well where the temperature changes suddenly. For this reason it is important to try to keep them where the temperature is stable and not to expose them to drafts.

Gerbils are capable of digesting a wide variety of foods, from seeds and plant matter to animal tissue, but they are also susceptible to digestive disorders. Foods that are too rich in fats and carbohydrates are not good for them, and a lack of roughage will also cause problems. Remember, roughage is necessary in a gerbil's diet just as in a person's diet. It is helpful in moving food through the digestive tract. Diarrhea may occur if too many soft vegetables are given to the gerbil.

Many of the same commonsense approaches to your own diet can be used with gerbils. You would not eat spoiled foods so you should not allow your gerbil to eat them either. Spoiled food is usually loaded with bacteria that can cause serious illness. If you give your gerbil fresh vegetables, be sure to remove uneaten portions before they spoil. This will also help

FACING PAGE:
This chinchilla male is beautiful and healthy.

Gerbils are naturally clean and will groom each other, as this black female and white male are doing.

keep the cage clean as well as preventing the animal from ingesting dangerous bacteria. Along the same lines of commonsense, storage of the food is very important to prevent spoilage and the possibility of chance of accidentally feeding bad food to your gerbil.

Gerbils that become ill do so because of poor management on the part of the owner. Keeping your gerbil healthy is your responsibility and is mostly a matter of common sense.

Illnesses

Preventive measures will greatly reduce the chance that your gerbil will become ill. Simple, common illnesses like colds can be prevented easily by keeping the gerbil warm and not exposing it to sudden temperature fluctuations and drafts. Keeping the cage dry will also help. Other respiratory problems can be avoided by changing the bedding often if you are using wood shavings since these break down into fine dust particles that, if inhaled constantly, cause respiratory disorders.

Other common disorders such as diarrhea are a product of a build-up of harmful bacteria in the digestive tract or a vitamin imbalance. The digestive tract is composed of certain varieties and proportions of bacteria known as the normal flora. An increase of certain species that leads to a skew in the proportions will cause diarrhea or other gastrointestinal disorders. These problems can be avoided by making sure the gerbils are not fed too many fresh green vegetables and that they are not allowed to eat food that has spoiled.

If your gerbil becomes sick, it will be fairly obvious by its behavior. Normally gerbils are very active and alert, responding with curiosity to things around them. Their fur will be soft and shiny and the eyes should be clear and bright. Anytime these signs are not present may indicate the gerbil is not healthy. A lethargic response to the introduction of something new to his environment would indicate that your gerbil may be ill. Loss of appetite is another good indicator of possible illness. Other illnesses such as the ones described earlier, like colds or diarrhea, are easily identifiable.

It is very important that your gerbil has hard materials to gnaw on. If these are not available its teeth will grow and cause severe damage to the animal. Rat food or dog biscuits from time to time are a good way to solve the problem. By checking your pet every day, you can easily identify problems early and treat them. If you do notice that your gerbil is sick, it is best to contact your veterinarian. The vet will suggest a change in diet or prescribe medication. Checking your gerbil daily will enable you to deal with most illnesses before they are too far along to treat.

SUMMARY

Gerbils are cute furry little rodents that make truly wonderful pets. Their natural habitats are the more arid regions of Asia and Africa. They are also the main focus of numerous research projects conducted by ecologists, physiologists, patho-physiologists, etc. Much of the interest in gerbils stems from their natural curiosity; in situations where most animals would retreat, these animals advance to investigate. They are fairly hardy with adaptive features which allow them to withstand varying climates.

Gerbils are small and care should be taken when han-

The main attraction of the gerbil is his curiosity and *joie de vivre*. The gerbil on the left is rising to look at something which caught his eye; on the right, this one is standing upright (note the visible scent gland which is used to mark territory).

dling them. They are very easy to house owing to their small size. A container with minimum dimensions of eight inches by eight inches by six inches high and ample ventilation is enough. A substrate that includes materials that can be shredded to make nest is also needed.

The diet of a gerbil, like all pets, must be given serious consideration. The most important thing is that it get a healthy variety of foods.

When choosing a gerbil it is important to make sure you select a healthy animal, especially if you intend to breed it. Breeding gerbils is not terribly difficult if they are maintained on a good diet and given ample space.

Like all pets, there is a chance that your gerbil may become ill. If this occurs the best thing to do is to contact your veterinarian. To avoid illness in your pets, be alert for any unusual behavior changes, feed and water them properly, and keep their cage clean.

This albino is a natural beauty in any setting. (It is not advisable to let *your* gerbil get too close to any houseplants, especially cacti.)

The following books by T.F.H. Publications are available at pet shops everywhere.

GERBILS: A COMPLETE INTRODUCTION—By Mrs. M. Ostrow
ISBN 0-86622-267-7
(Hardcover) **TFH CO-018**
ISBN 0-86622-299-5
(Softcover) **TFH CO-018S**
Great four-color drawings and photos combine with a prac-

SUGGESTED READING

tical and easy-to-read text to make a book of pure enchantment for beginning gerbils fanciers.
128 pages, 5½ x 8½; Contains 93 full-color photos and 8 full-color line drawings.

THE ENCYCLOPEDIA OF GERBILS—By D. Robinson
ISBN 0-87666-915-1 **TFH H-974**
Contents: This book covers the set-up and Maintenance of Housing Facilities, Handling, Feeding, Breeding, and Care of Gerbils. It is also a comprehensive guide to the gerbil's characteristics and behavior.
Audience: Written for either amateur or professional keepers, especially valuable for beginners.
Hard cover; 8 x 5½; 224 pages 57 full-color photos, 102 black and white photos.

GERBILS—By Paul Paradise
ISBN 0-87666-927-5 **TFH KW-037**
This 96-page hardcover book is chock full of good advice and good photos: it covers what a beginner really needs to know.
40 full-color photos; 30 black and white photos.

Index